Barricades Burning

Barricades Burning
Political and Personal Poems

Eric Leif Davin

DavinBooks
Box 90087
Pittsburgh, Pennsylvania 15224

Barricades Burning

Political and Personal Poems

Front Cover:
Barricades Burning in Kiev

The Political is Personal

Barricades Burning

Crassus crucified Spartacus,
And lined the Appian Way
With dead gladiators.
But when he assembled his armies
To conquer the East,
One Roman stood alone
At the gates of Rome
And called down the wrath of the gods
On the conquering legions
As they marched out.
The legions died at Carrhae,
And the King of Parthia
Poured molten gold
Down the throat of Crassus.

The Zealots died at Masada
As Rome
Tore down the walls of Jerusalem,
Burned the Temple,
And dispersed the Jews.
But the Goths burned Rome.

Joan fought for France at Orleans.
The English burned her at the stake,
But the Church made her a saint.

Galileo claimed the earth moved.
The Inquisition forced him to recant.
        "But nevertheless,"
                He said
                        When released,
"The earth moves."

Freedom died in Budapest.
Spring died in Prague and Damascus.
But one man stood alone
        Against the tanks in Beijing,
And Mandela walked free
        In Johannesburg.

The Cossacks
        Whipped the girls in Sochi,
But still,
        As the whips came down,
                The girls sang.
And in Kiev,
        The barricades burned.

Power Never Sleeps

Bodies writhe on the bed,
Locked in mortal combat,
Wrestling on a battlefield
Where Power fucks,
But Power never sleeps.
Power prowls
In the trenches of the family.
Power howls
In the trenches of the schools.
Power lurks
In the trenches of the church.
Power shills
In the trenches of the corporation.
And Power kills
In the trenches of the city.
But Power never sleeps.
Power destroys the village
To save the village.
Power enshrines privilege
In the name of freedom.
Power says it's for the best,
But it's for the worst.
Power seeps into our heads,
And Power creeps into our beds...
But Power never sleeps.

Class

It is the invisible reality
Which grinds you in its fist
Without mercy or pity
From your first cry
To the day you die.
But you swear it doesn't exist.

It is everywhere
And nowhere.
You can't touch it,
But it touches you.
You don't see it,
But it sees you.
It is confusion
And illusion.

And behind its veil
Is Harvard and Yale
Or a life in jail.
Nob Hill
Or New Orleans.
Polo dreams
Or bowling teams.
Ladies in waiting
Or beer and tailgating.

It's your last known address
        And whether you get redress.
It's where you went to school
        And if they play you for a fool.
It's the amount of your wealth
        And the quality of your health.
It's how well you know Macbeth
        And the date of your death.

        But you swear it doesn't exist.

Be Afraid

Of the people over here,
    And the people over there,
The dark-skinned mother,
    And your own blood brother,
Of the red in your bed,
    And people everywhere.

Be afraid of your shadow,
    And kids in the schools
        Who might be packing guns.
Of the man with the beard
    And people looking weird,
Of the graveyard ghosts
    And the people on the Coast,
        Be afraid of the nuns!

Be afraid
Of the short and afraid of the tall,
Of just about any damn one at all
    Who doesn't look like you,
    And doesn't cook like you,
Doesn't drink like you,
    And doesn't think like you.

Trust only in the Lord,
And the brute in the suit
Pointing his finger
At the people over there,
And the people over here
At the straight and the queer
And people everywhere,

Telling you
Ya gotta,
Ya gotta
Ya gotta be afraid,
Ya gotta be afraid,
Ya gotta be very, very afraid.

Fossil Fools

Great gulping gas hogs,
Bought with instant loans,
Guzzle at the nozzle
And bestride the land,
Devouring dinosaur bones
From beneath the sand.

With swag sucked from the soil
Beneath our feet,
Oil-sucking vampire lords
Swagger in their insolent chariots,
Filling the street
With the racing riots
Of their vermin hoards.

So this is the way the world ends:
In a paradise for parasites.
Laughing at our sorrow,
They drink the future
Like there's no tomorrow.

Laughing at their sins,
They are confident
That even God will relent,
Will not condemn
Their mayhem
And will let them
Buy their way into heaven.

But they're driving their coffins.
Let them lie where they die.

The Wealthy & The Wretched

The wealthy own the rich wide lands
While the wretched work
With calloused hands.
The wealthy praise their own misdeeds,
While the wretched eat
Their woeful weeds.
The wealthy frolic wild and free,
While the wretched clear away
The debris.

They may be callow fools
And knaves,
But the wealthy have their pools
And slaves,
While the wretched have their graves.

Hell House

The crack house
Festers on its junkyard lot
Like an open sore,
A poison spring
Polluting every pore
Of our lives
With its human sewage.

The crack house
Is a flophouse
Of ruined lives
And broken hopes,
A cesspool of fools
And dope maggots.

The crack house
Is a crack cancer,
Spreading its fingers
Into all who linger,
Rotting their bodies,
Blighting their minds,
Eating their souls
Like a death dancer.

The crack house
Is the Mouth of Hell,
Through which
Demons swell
In human form
And are vomited upon the world.

And from the crack house
Few return.
It is the Gate to Hell
...And the Devil guards it well.

In the Land of the Free

Bums are babbling
    On the highways and byways,
Communing with the Cosmos,
    In the Land of the Free.

Begging for pennies,
    Begging for nickles,
        Begging for dimes,
            Spare change,
        Any change at all
    In the Land of the Free.

Everywhere in the Land of the Free
    There are bums who are free
        To beg,
            To starve,
                Free to stagger
    Through another cold night,
        To sleep under bridges
            In the winter twilight.

We stumble over
The stumble bums
Begging for a handout
Or a helping hand,
Begging for scraps
In the Land of the Free.

Bums, in their rotting clothes,
Cleaning our windshields
When we stop for the light.
Bums, with their hands
Caked with filth,
Holding open doors
At all the big stores,
Anything to make themselves useful
For a quarter or two.

Bums, with their rotting teeth,
Eating from dumpsters,
Filling the soup kitchens
Which are filling the cities
Of the Land of the Free.

Bums puking at bus stops
In the noon day sun,
Bums crawling into alleys
In the putrid night,

Crawling into fatal fetal positions,
As if to crawl back
Into their mothers' bellies.

Bums in the gutter,
Muttering to demons,
And bums on the airwaves,
Howling like demons
At the bums in the gutter.

Bums on park benches
And bums on court benches,
Spewing their venom
At the bums on park benches.

Everywhere in the Land of the Free
There are bums in low places
And bums in high places.
Bums in the board rooms,
And bums in the Congress,
Bums in the Senate,
And bums in the White House.

And the more bums there are
In the high places of power,
The more bums there are
In the Land of the Free.

Every Five Days

The sign said,
"Every five days in this state
A woman is dead,
Beaten to death
By her husband,
The father of her children,
Her boyfriend,
Or her lover.
Every five days."

And every day
One is beaten near to death
Just for living.

And every second day
One wishes for death
Because she is *still* living.

And every third day,
Every bruise,
Every scar,
Every broken bone
Reminds one that her broken home

Is just a Hell House
In which she is trapped
Every fourth day
In a dead end life
Which will only end
For this desperate housewife...

Every fifth day.

In Ateleta, November, 1943

"The Germans went
From house to house,"
Umberto said.
"After that, all were dead."

Italian winter turned roads to mud
Along the Sangro,
Along Blood River,
And in Ateleta,
A town of blood.
And high on the mountains above,
Behind their barbed wire
And their guns,
Perched the Germans,
Looking down
On Blood River
And the town of blood.
...And one of them was missing.

"And so the Germans came down
To our town,
And went from house to house,"
Vincenzo said.
"They took my father," Ida said.

"And they took my mother,"
said Maria.
"Shc was looking for a cow,
And they took her to the wall.
They took the boy next door,
Who hadn't run away
Like all the other boys.
They took whole families,
Babies too,
And lined them all
Against the wall."

Then German guns turned
On all the old men,
The old women,
And the children,
Standing in the mud,
Against the wall,
In Ateleta,
On Blood River.

The Jewish Cobbler

Panzers poured across the border.
He obeyed the order
To saddle up and ride.
And so they died,
Ground beneath the wheel
Of blitzkrieg German steel.
But this Polish Jew
Was one of few
Who spoke
Without a traitor trace
The language of the Master Race.
And so they let him stay
Among the servile ranks,
Making more
Of the hated panzer tanks.
And when, in time,
His monster masters strutted
Down the line,
It was he who guided them,
Delighted them,
With the way he made
The hated panzer tanks.

And so they let him stay,
Till there was no one
To denounce him,
Or renounce him,
To strip away his careful lies,
When he let his monster masters
Think that he
Was one of them.

But those are ancient days, he said
Under distant skies,
And most I knew
Are long-since dead,
Including all the Jews.

So, now, here in my dingy den,
Instead of making panzer tanks,
I gladly take your thanks
For patching up your shoes.

Santa Ana's Leg

Oh, it's really such a bore,
    How Santa Ana lost his leg
In the silly Pastry War.

But he buried it in style,
    With pomp and poetry,
Beneath a fancy pile.

Later, when the peons tossed him out,
    They dug up Santa Ana's leg
And kicked it all about.

But Santa Ana didn't care,
    He had a cork and wooden leg
He wore most everywhere.

Then the gringos came on down
    To find old Santa Ana
And run him out of town.

He fled so fast he left behind
    The cork and wooden leg
He hoped the gringos wouldn't find.

But the gringos quickly found
    Santa Ana's wooden leg
And passed it all around.

Then they brought it home
    And sent it out on tour
From Miami up to Nome.

Every state and county fair
    Hosted Santa Ana's leg,
While the gringos came to stare.

'Til at last it ceased to roam
    In Springfield, Illinois,
Which became its final home.

It lies there still, all brown and dull,
    Santa Ana's wooden leg,
In the state capitol.

What a strange trophy of war,
    The cork and wooden leg
That Santa Ana wore.

The Cry of the Suffering People

The suffering people lift their eyes
To the looming skies
And cry to Heaven above
To send them a Salvador Mundi,
A Savior of the World.

The suffering people want to know,
Who is the New Messiah?
The Chosen One?
The Anointed One?
The One Foretold?
Who will save us
From the Dark Satanic Power
That has spread its malignant hand
All across the land?

Is it Bernie?
Then we will vote Red.
Is it Uncle Joe,
Risen again from the dead?
Then we will vote the status quo.

We just want to know,
We just want to be led.

Who is the New Messiah?
Who is the Savior,
Come to deliver us from Evil?

Tell us so we know,
Which way does the wind blow?
Tell us, O, tell us,
Who do we follow?
How do we vote?
Tell us so we know,
Who is the Most Electable
In all the land?

Tell us so we know.

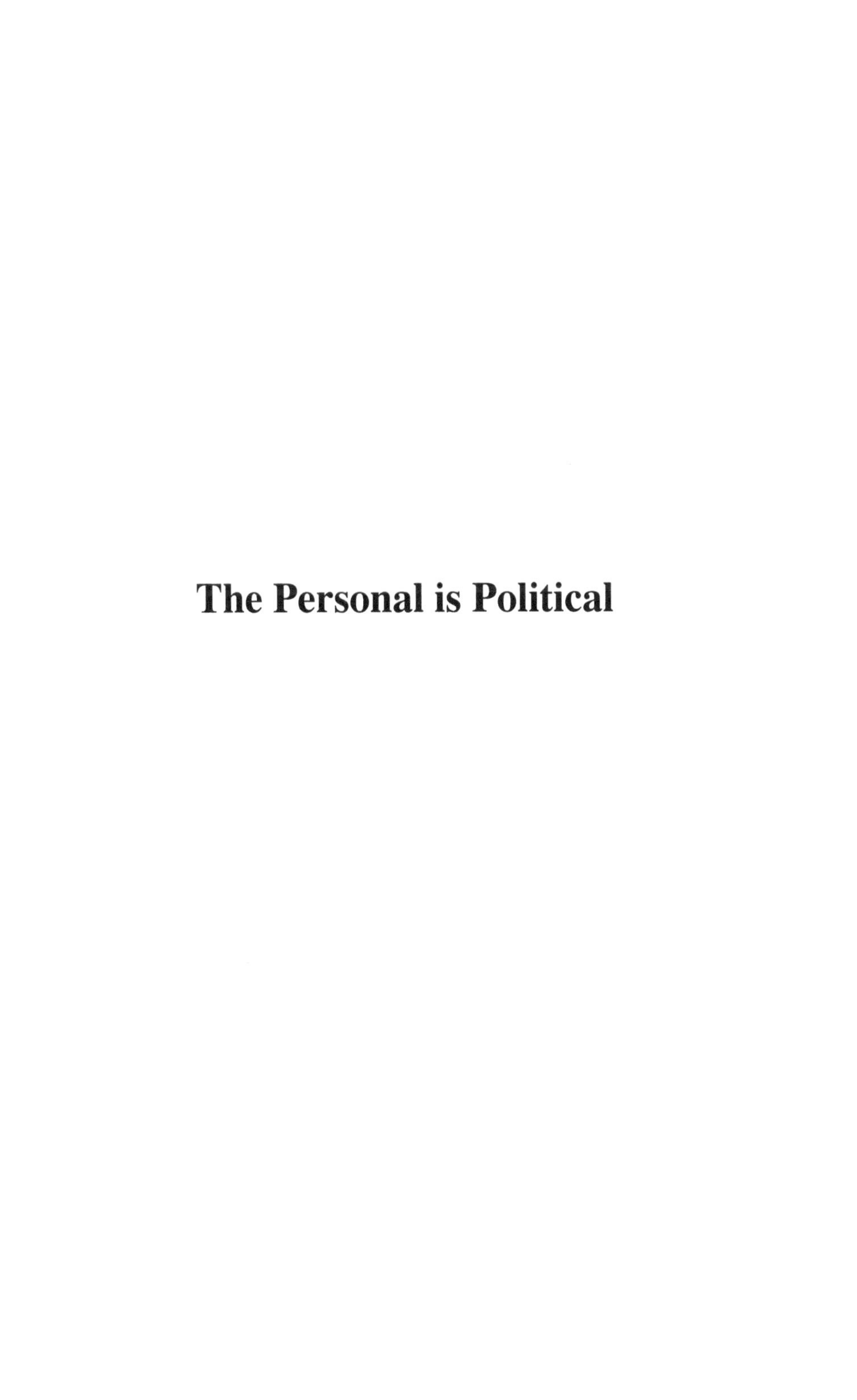

The Personal is Political

St. Patrick's Day Lament

There are no buds upon the trees,
No smiles in Irish eyes,
There are no hints of laden breeze,
No sign of summer sighs,
But only froth of snowfalls past
Which lies and lies
Like dragonflies
In amber cast.

The Mayfly's Love Song

Our love is eternal,
  As we flit among the flowers,
'Til the seconds become minutes,
  And the minutes become hours,

'Til the sun ends its flight
  And settles in the West,
'Til the day becomes the night.
  Our love will stand the test.

Zeus on the Loose

Zeus, how did Hera stand you?
You never could be true.
You were always after
Some shepherd girl,
Some nubile nymph,
Some lovely Leda.

And Hera, patient Hera,
Always waited for you to return.
Not with the patience of Penelope,
This is true.
She did not forgive
Your lusty rompings
Among the peons and the peasants.
She did not forget
The poor girls
You seduced and abandoned.
But she always took you back.

And what was it
With all the beastiality?
Couldn't you get it up as a man?

Take lovely Leda
(Which you did).
She merely came to admire
The beauty of the swan.

But it was you,
Hidden beneath the feathers,
Waiting for your chance
To swan dive
Between her legs.

Lovely Leda never would have
Made it with a swan.
What made her lose it
With a bird?
Your animal magnetism?

I could understand
Why Europa fell for you.
You came on to her
Like a bull in heat.
No wonder
She climbed on top of you
And took you for a ride.
But you left her, too.
That was your style.

You were hung,
But you didn't hang.
In and out.
Here today,
Gone tomorrow.
Wouldn't bother
To come again.

And the litter of kittens,
The gaggle of geese,
The clutch of chicks
You left behind?
Not your concern.

You had your own worries, Zeus.
Hera was waiting for you,
With her favorite dish:
Cooked goose.

Birds of a Feather

Packed tight, like beads on a string,
Birds perched on the wire.
More lit,
And the birds,
Jostling, flapping, complaining,
Bumped down the wire.

And then they were gone,
A flickering cloud,
Fading away.

Clouds

Stark balls of cotton,
Bold in the shocking blue sky,
Solid as the Earth.

Night Birds

Iced night birds huddle
In their dry, dark, feather nests.
After long flight -- Home.

Spring

Ice on the water.
Beside the dark stream moonlight
Bathes the first flower.

My Native Land

My native land was the Cracker South,
Land of swamps and skeeters
And Ol' Man River.
Good Ol' Boys
Who gave the Rebel Yell,
Held the noose,
And grew strange fruit
In the Southern breeze.
Proud descendants of Dixieland,
Who bled and died
In the Civil War,
For the White Man's land,
And the land of the Klan.

Mom Played Ball

Mom played ball in blackface.
    All the Southern girls did.
        She didn't know why.
Maybe so her Southern kin
    Could laugh
At girls playing ball like boys,
    And Darkies playing ball like men.

Her Last Reading
Anne Sexton at Harvard
March 7, 1974

She stands alone,
Thin and bony in the light,
Her manuscript before her on the lectern
As she whispers
Into the microphone.
In times past a jazz trio stood beside her,
The deep bass
Punctuating the words
As the mournful horn
Lovingly caressed her poems.
But tonight she stands alone,
Thin and bony in the light,
Still only part way back from Bedlam,
Her awful rowing toward God
Near the end.
Tonight, the Pulitzer cannot save her,
The trio cannot save her.
The audience,
Silent as the grave,
Cannot save her
As, for the last time,
She reads her suicide notes.

She sucks death from her cigarettes,
Her head wreathed
In billowing clouds,
That form
A swirling nimbus
Around her dark form.
But they were too slow.
Six months later
She found a faster way.
Her car's exhaust.

SALSA SOUL

Beads of sweat on a bare black belly.
Soul Sister swaying
To the Salsa beat
In the Latin heat
Of a hot August night.

Beads of sweat on a lean black belly.
Salsa Soul,
Black as coal,
Black as night,
Black & hot
As the August night.

Beads of sweat on a bare black belly.
African soul in Latin heat.
Hips moving
To the Salsa beat.

Beads of sweat
On a hot August night.

Circe

It is not your glance,
It is not your walk,
It is not your word
That unleashes the beast.
It is the sorcery of your touch.

You touch me,
And I am no longer human.
You touch me,
And I am an animal
Straining at my leash.
You touch me,
And I am a monster,
Raging in my lust.
You touch me,
And I am Ariel in love,
Grendel in pain.
You touch me,
And I howl in the dust.
You touch me...
And I am your beast.

Talons

Your diamond talons,
    Sharper than a panther's claws,
Leave scarlet trails
    Down my back,
A cicatrix of fire
    To mark your passion and desire.

Hold My Heart Gently

I am here.
Seek me.
Hear me.
Draw near me in the darkness.

Hold my heart gently
In your healing hands.
For my heart is far from home.
I have been
Swimming with the Sharks,
Running with the Wolves,
Sleeping with the Enemy.
And now
My heart hunts alone
Through the dark
And wounded lands.

Draw near me in the darkness.
Hold my heart gently
In your healing hands.

I Don’t Know Why

I don’t know why
    I dance stark naked
        In the midnight flames.
I don’t know why
    I chase the shadows in the mist
        Raise my fist
            Against the angry sky.
I don’t know why
    I fight the fiery angels,
        Shake my chains,
            Carry these scars
        And howl in pain
    Beneath the distant stars.
        I don’t know why.

The Wandering Jew

I am in the world,
        But not of the world.
I am lost in the ozone,
        Flying beneath the radar,
Neither this nor that,
        Neither Yin nor Yang.
I am the intimate stranger,
        In a strange land.
I know the rules
        That do not bind me.
I know the names
        That do not name me.
I now the customs and rituals
        Of friends and lovers,
                Sisters and brothers,
Of families that do not call me home.
I am the visitor to the lodge,
        The tourist out of season,
                The reporter on assignment.
I walk among the natives,
        The familiar anthropologist,
                Received and accepted.
I am the chanter in the dark,
        The dancer in the firelight,
Gone native, I am a member of the tribe.

I am the White African,
    The Indian Cowboy,
        The Female Man.
            The Hebrew Goy.
I celebrate both Christmas,
    And Chanukkah,
        The Winter Solstice,
    And the Festival of the Lights.

I am the Wandering Jew
    Wondering,
        As I wander,
If the Messiah will ever come.

Bless me, Father, for I have sinned.
    Hail Mary, full of grace,
Blessed art thou,
    And the fruit of they womb,
        Jesus.

Blessed Jesus, walk with me,
    Next year,
        In Jerusalem.

That Dark and Lonely Hill

There is a dark and lonely hill.
And we live in sorrow
Beneath that dark and lonely hill.
Because we live in time.

And where there is time,
There is loss.
And where there is loss,
There is sorrow.
And so we live in sorrow
Beneath that dark and lonely hill.
And, in time,
All must climb
That dark and lonely hill.
Rich man, poor man,
Beggar man, thief.
The Prince and the Pauper,
The Commander-in-Chief,
The whore and the lady,
Madonna and Child,
The good, the bad,
The meek and the mild.
In time,
All must climb,
That dark and lonely hill.

We Are Mistaken

We think space is finite.
    But it is infinite.
        We think our lives infinite.
            But they are finite.

And all too soon,
    Like a dying moon,
        We age and fade
            Into the night,
        No matter how much we rage
    Against the dying of the light.

Come From the Shadows

Reach out of the darkness,
Take my hand,
And come from the shadows
For you are not alone.

I have not forgotten you.
I know your name,
I know your story.
I remember everything,
And I have come for you.

I will roll away the stone
And lift you from the depths.
I will take the weight that you carry,
And dry the tears from your face.

I will give you a reason to believe
That yesterday's gone.
The dark night is over,
There is light in the distance,
It is the coming of the dawn.

The Way

Alone, the scholar
Embraces the universe,
Content in silence.

www.ingramcontent.com/pod-product-compliance
Ingram Content Group UK Ltd.
Pitfield, Milton Keynes, MK11 3LW, UK
UKHW040028200726
13854UKWH00001B/408

9 781365 048807